ISBN 978-0-265-02783-7
PIBN 10958842

1 MONTH OF
FREE
READING

at

www.ForgottenBooks.com

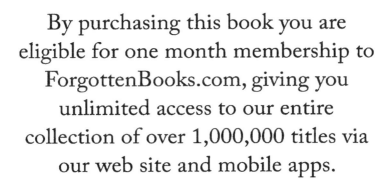

By purchasing this book you are eligible for one month membership to ForgottenBooks.com, giving you unlimited access to our entire collection of over 1,000,000 titles via our web site and mobile apps.

To claim your free month visit:

www.forgottenbooks.com/free958842

English
Français
Deutsche
Italiano
Español
Português

www.forgottenbooks.com

Mythology Photography **Fiction**
Fishing Christianity **Art** Cooking
Essays Buddhism Freemasonry
Medicine **Biology** Music **Ancient**
Egypt Evolution Carpentry Physics
Dance Geology **Mathematics** Fitness
Shakespeare **Folklore** Yoga Marketing
Confidence Immortality Biographies
Poetry **Psychology** Witchcraft
Electronics Chemistry History **Law**
Accounting **Philosophy** Anthropology
Alchemy Drama Quantum Mechanics
Atheism Sexual Health **Ancient History**
Entrepreneurship Languages Sport
Paleontology Needlework Islam
Metaphysics Investment Archaeology
Parenting Statistics Criminology
Motivational

Prospects

for

Foreign

Trade in

DAIRY CATTLE AND DAIRY AND POULTRY PRODUCTS

Foreign Agricultural Service
UNITED STATES DEPARTMENT OF AGRICULTURE

APRIL 1964

CONTENTS

PROSPECTS FOR FOREIGN TRADE IN DAIRY CATTLE AND DAIRY AND POULTRY PRODUCTS

POULTRY AND POULTRY PRODUCTS

Prospects for U.S. exports of poultry meat appear to be developing in new markets of the Far East, Africa, and Latin America, as well as in the Western Hemisphere and Europe. The rate at which this increased demand will expand is in large measure dependent upon progress made in raising individual income levels. All indications point to a larger production of eggs and poultry meat in 1964. Only a small increase in output of eggs appears likely, but production of broilers and turkeys is expected to expand considerably. In view of recent developments and the current rate of U.S. exports, it is expected that trade in 1964 will be maintained at about the same level as in 1963. Under present trading conditions, a resumption of the sharp upward trend prevailing during the 1957-62 period is highly improbable.

CURRENT WORLD SITUATION

In 1963, world production of poultry and eggs was slightly higher than in 1962. Increases in egg production were limited mainly to the less developed countries. However, production in the United States, by far the largest Free World producer, rose 1 percent, while that of the United Kingdom, the second largest producer, averaged slightly higher than a year earlier.

A large part of the world's poultry meat continues to be a by-product of the small farm flock kept for egg production. Until a few years ago, poultry meat production could be expected to follow closely the level of chicken numbers and egg production in most countries. As a result of the outstanding success of the United States in producing broilers of excellent quality on a large scale at low cost, many other countries are adopting similar poultry-meat production practices. Among countries which now have a well-advanced broiler industry are Canada, the United Kingdom, the Netherlands, Denmark, France, West Germany, Belgium, Australia, and Mexico. In most of these countries, chicken numbers reported on a particular census date do not accurately reflect the dimensions of the broiler industry. In some countries, the number of broilers being raised are excluded in counting the poultry population. While statistics of poultry meat are available for only a few countries, including the United States, Canada, European Economic Community (EEC) countries, Denmark, and the United Kingdom, pronounced increases have been reported in these countries. The United States is by far the largest producer of poultry meat. United States consumption of poultry meat is very high-- about 39 pounds per capita. In 1963, only about 3 percent of total U.S. production of poultry meat was exported, compared with 4 percent in 1962. Other principal exporting countries were Denmark and the Netherlands, with France and Belgium making substantial gains under the protective tariff set up recently by the EEC.

INTERNATIONAL TRADE

Poultry Meat

International trade in poultry meat declined sharply in 1963. Imports by West Germany, the principal market, were 379 million pounds, down over 20 percent from the record 469 million pounds shipped in 1962. Germany's imports from most major suppliers were off, but shipments from non-EEC countries, mainly the United States and Denmark, declined most. Consumers, impressed with the improved quality of ready-to-cook chicken, increased per capita consumption from about 6 pounds in 1958 to over 12 pounds in 1962. However, a rise in poultry meat prices in Germany, after imposition of higher Common Market duty rates on third-country imports, has temporarily arrested the rapid rate of increase in per capita consumption.

During 1963, the United States continued to make representations to the EEC to lower its duties on poultry meat which had been increased from 15.9 percent ad valorem before July 31, 1962, to the equivalent of about 45 percent ad valorem by 1963. Major actions taken by the United States during 1963 in an attempt to obtain some adjustment in the restrictive levies include the following:

During the first six months of 1963, the U.S. government made repeated requests to the EEC for reductions in the gate price and variable levies on U.S. poultry products.

After these efforts proved unsuccessful, the United States, on July 25, 1963, began negotiations with the EEC under the special bilateral agreement arrived at in 1962. These negotiations resulted in no mutually satisfactory arrangement concerning levies imposed on imported poultry meat.

On August 7, 1963, the United States indicated its intention to withdraw tariff concessions on items previously negotiated with the EEC or Member States, having a trade value equivalent to the estimated level of trade the United States ascribed to its poultry trade. Substantial doubts were raised by the EEC regarding the value of this trade. Consequently, it was agreed that a panel would be appointed to arbitrate the disputed trade value.

On October 29, 1963, the Council of Representatives to the General Agreement on Tariffs and Trade (GATT) appointed a panel to render an advisory opinion on the value to be ascribed, as of September 1, 1960, to exports of U.S. poultry meat to West Germany.

The panel held a number of meetings during the period November 11-19, 1963, to review written submissions from the two parties to the dispute and to hear oral presentations.

On November 21, 1963, the committee announced its advisory opinion. In brief, the opinion rendered was that a figure of $26 million would reasonably represent the value to be ascribed as of September 1, 1960, to U.S. exports of poultry meat to West Germany.

On December 4, 1963, the U.S. Government notified the General Secretary of GATT that tariff concessions on brandy, certain trucks, dextrine and

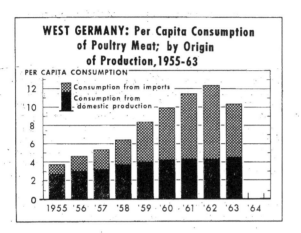

WEST GERMANY: Per Capita Consumption of Poultry Meat; by Origin of Production, 1955-63

PER CAPITA CONSUMPTION

Consumption from imports

Consumption from domestic production

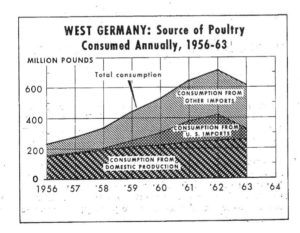

WEST GERMANY: Source of Poultry Consumed Annually, 1956-63

MILLION POUNDS

Total consumption

CONSUMPTION FROM OTHER IMPORTS

CONSUMPTION FROM U. S. IMPORTS

CONSUMPTION FROM DOMESTIC PRODUCTION

starches would be withdrawn as of January 7, 1964, when the higher duties in effect before the concession would be reinstated. This withdrawal of approximately $26 million in tariff concessions was taken to restore the balance of tariff concessions between the United States and the EEC, which had been upset by the higher levies on U.S. poultry exports to West Germany.

Eggs

World trade in eggs decreased substantially in 1963. As in the case of poultry, Western Europe accounts for over 75 percent of the total trade, with West Germany the largest market. West German imports of eggs were down over 25 percent from their 1962 level. While most of the reduction was in purchases from the Netherlands, those from Denmark fell by over 40 percent. Polish shipments were less than one third their 1962 level. On the other hand, there was a substantial rise in receipts from France and some increase in purchases from Bulgaria, Czechoslovakia, Finland, and Hungary. Egg product imports were also down, as supplies from the United States and Yugoslavia were reduced considerably. Trade in shell eggs and egg products has been clouded recently by higher import duties and other trade restrictions. The situation was further compounded by the EEC Commission action on October 7, 1963, and on January 20, 1964, placing supplemental levies on dried whole eggs, dried and frozen yolk, and shell eggs. These levies were in addition to the variable levies already being charged on these products. The purpose of the virtually prohibitive levy on dried eggs remains obscure, as there were no additional processing facilities within the EEC to supply market requirements for dried egg products. If the increased duties remain in force, it can be expected that third-country suppliers, mainly Denmark and the United States, will experience a decline in trade with this major market.

UNITED STATES IN THE WORLD SITUATION

Poultry Meat

The rapid developments in international trade in poultry and egg products in the last year culminated in a sharp decline in U.S. exports of frozen poultry in 1963. This is contrasted with substantial increases in exports of canned poultry, of hatching, shell, and dried eggs, and of baby chicks.

In 1962, U.S. shipments of poultry meat went to about 70 countries and independent territories and were valued at $76 million. In 1963, the value of our meat exports dropped to $57 million. Aside from small amounts moved under Public Law 480, Title I agreements, all U.S. exports of poultry products constitute dollar sales and move through regular commercial channels without benefit of any subsidy.

The major markets for U.S. poultry meat changed somewhat in 1963. U.S. trade with Germany and the Netherlands was off sharply; however, these continued to be our largest markets. Greece, which took only 3.1 million pounds in 1962, was third in 1963, accounting for 16.5 million pounds. Spectacular growth was also experienced in the Japanese market, which imported

9.6 million pounds in 1963. Other major markets continued to be Switzerland, Hong Kong, and Canada.

Markets for U.S. poultry result largely from production efficiencies and a consciously planned program of consumer education and promotion, carried out cooperatively in importing countries by the U.S. poultry industry and the Foreign Agricultural Service. This market promotion program operates most actively in five Western European countries and in Japan.

The accessibility and growing popularity of U.S. frozen poultry meat of all kinds undoubtedly has been an important factor in stimulating the recent rapid expansion of international trade in this product. The ability of the United States to market poultry competitively throughout the world has been an important factor in efforts abroad to increase and improve poultry meat production and marketing methods.

With the implementation of EEC poultry regulations in August 1962, the phenomenal growth of U.S. poultry exports evidenced during recent years was brought to an abrupt halt. In West Germany, our major market, import duties have now tripled. U.S. exports to West Germany in 1963 were only 75 million pounds, down 50 percent from a year earlier. Total U.S. exports of poultry meat in 1963 totaled 208.8 million pounds.

Broilers and fryers continued to be the leading export commodity, accounting for about half of the value of poultry meat exports. The value of U.S. poultry meat exports in 1963 reached $56.8 million, of which $28.2 million was derived from trade in broilers and fryers. In terms of volume, exports of broilers and fryers were down in 1963 even more sharply, 112.3 million pounds compared with 172.6 million in 1962.

Demand for canned poultry increased sharply in 1963. This was to a considerable extent caused by the increased prices of other poultry products in Western Europe. During 1962, U.S. exports of canned poultry to the EEC totaled 3.5 million pounds. With implementation of the EEC levy system and consequently higher consumer prices for fresh and frozen poultry meat, U.S. exports of canned poultry to the EEC more than doubled. Exports to the EEC in 1963 totaled 8.7 million pounds. If the present degree of protection afforded EEC poultry continues, demand for canned poultry will probably remain strong.

U.S. exports of turkey in 1963 were 84 percent of the record 1962 level. In 1963, exports were 30.9 million pounds compared with the 36.9 million shipped in 1962. The major market continued to be West Germany, which accounted for over 60 percent of the trade.

Live Poultry and Eggs

Trade in eggs and egg products, production stock, and other live poultry were up sharply from a total export value of $20.5 million in 1962 to about $28.7 million in 1963.

U.S. exports of live poultry showed substantial gains in 1963. Total exports of baby chicks amounted to 27.2 million head, surpassing the record

high of 25.5 million head set in 1961, and up 40 percent over the 1962 level.
The major buyer continued to be Canada, accounting for over one-third of
the trade. Other major markets, in order of importance, were Mexico,
Dominican Republic, Italy, Spain, and Japan.

Other live poultry exports, including turkey poults, ducklings, etc., were
up sharply in 1963. Trade in 1963 amounted to 4 million pounds, up 45 percent
from the 1962 level.

U.S. exports of hatching, shell, and dried eggs were up substantially in
1963, but exports of frozen eggs were less than half their 1962 level.

Exports of market (shell) eggs showed the greatest increase, with 1963
trade reaching 7.7 million dozen. This increase halted, temporarily, the
downward trend, which started in 1956, in exports of market eggs. The
major outlets for U.S. market eggs continued to be the Netherlands Antilles
and Canada. However, because of the severe winter in Europe and a tem-
porary shortage of eggs, U.S. exports to that area increased substantially.
Most of these eggs moved during the early months of 1963, when U.S. prices
were low. Switzerland, which normally imports negligible quantities, took
over 2 million dozen in 1963. Shipments to France and Spain were also up.
Canada, long a major U.S. market, also took substantially larger quantities.
A decrease in Canadian egg production in early 1963, resulting from a sizable
reduction in the laying flock, made it necessary for that country to increase
its 1963 imports. The outlook for 1964, however, is not as bright. It can be
expected that U.S. eggs will again encounter keen price competition in world
markets and that as a result export trade, barring any unusual developments,
is not expected to be maintained at the 1963 level.

Prospects for hatching eggs are more favorable. U.S. exports of hatching
eggs increased from 6.8 million dozen in 1962 to 9.9 million dozen in 1963.
The major markets continued to be Canada and Venezuela, accounting for
about 75 percent of total U.S. exports. Shipments to Canada doubled as total
hatchings were up nearly 6 percent. Canada's entire hatch increase was in
broiler-type chicks.

U.S. exports of dried eggs were moderately higher. Slightly more than
5 million pounds were shipped in 1963 compared with 4.3 million pounds
in 1962. West Germany, United Kingdom, and Switzerland continued to be
leading markets. The severe winter in Europe, and the inability of the Community's egg products industry to supply the market, were important factors
contributing to demand for U.S. dried eggs. Shipments would have been larger
if higher duties had not been levied on dried egg product imports into the
EEC, our major market.

The decline in U.S. exports of frozen eggs in 1963 can be attributed
largely to the higher EEC duties charged third-country suppliers, forcing
more intra-Community trade. In 1962, West Germany accounted for over
50 percent of total U.S. trade in frozen eggs. Upon implementation of the CAP
on poultry products in August 1962, and additional supplemental levies in
1963, duties on frozen eggs were more than tripled, thus eliminating the
competitive position of the United States. If these increased duties remain in
force, it can be expected that U.S. trade in egg products will be sharply cur-
tailed in 1964.

BUILDING WORLD MARKETS

Promotional Activity

On-the-spot surveys were conducted by poultry marketing specialists to evaluate markets and to recommend programs and procedures designed to broaden marketing opportunities in Europe, Latin America, and the Far East. Work was also carried out in support of the more intensive promotional program of the Institute of American Poultry Industries (IAPI), the FAS cooperator representing the U.S. poultry industry in Western Europe, and promising markets of the Far East and Latin America.

Special promotional efforts were initiated in Far Eastern markets, principally Japan and Hong Kong. Spectacular growth was evidenced in Japan following promotional activity, culminating in the Tokyo Trade Center show held in September 1963. U.S. exports to Japan in 1963 amounted to almost 10 million pounds compared with shipments of less than 1 million pounds in 1962. Greece was another market where promotional efforts paid off. Trade with that country in 1963 totaled 16.5 million pounds, up sharply from the 3.1 million pounds shipped in 1962.

Recently, Peru lowered its import duties on dressed poultry reestablishing the U.S. competitive position in the market. It is hopeful that an effective local program can be worked out to further increase the sales of U.S. poultry in that country. Of special interest was the extent to which larger purchases of U.S. dressed poultry, by increasing demand, had benefited the local poultry industry.

Participation in Meetings

Foreign Agricultural Service activities included participation in numerous national association activities and international poultry meetings. For example, representatives of the Division were program participants at the Southeastern Poultry and Egg Association and the Pacific Dairy and Poultry Association Conventions. Representatives also participated in the annual Fact-Finding Conference discussing export problems and prospects of future trade. This type of activity serves the industry by keeping it advised of the problems of exporting its products, and by outlining procedures and methods to expand exports.

Overcoming Dollar Shortages

Current U.S. poultry and egg export markets have not been materially affected by dollar shortages. This problem is a major consideration in many potential or prospective markets, particularly in the newly independent countries of Africa. Although use has been made of Public Law 480, Title I (sales for local currencies) and economic aid programs in moving poultry and eggs, in 1963, only about 11 million pounds of poultry meat was moved under Title I. Frozen and canned poultry was programmed to the Republic of Congo, the UAR, and a small amount to Pakistan. In many of the developing countries, poultry meat is considered a luxury item and marketing and distribution facilities are not sufficiently advanced to handle the frozen or canned product satisfactorily.

Lessening Trade Barriers

Foreign countries continue to maintain old restrictions and barriers and to adopt new trade-inhibiting practices which limit imports of poultry and poultry products from the United States. Notable examples of maintaining highly restrictive practices can be found in countries of South America, with the exception of Peru and Surinam. All others preclude poultry imports by one method or another. Some ban imports because Newcastle disease is endemic in the United States. Others require import licenses which are virtually impossible to obtain. Some issue licenses only if the importer is willing to pay a premium.

In Europe, several countries restrict imports of U.S. poultry because of Newcastle disease. These include Ireland, the United Kingdom, Norway, Sweden and Denmark. France refuses to permit U.S. imports because the United States does not ban the feeding of certain oestrogens and arsenicals.

To cope with these many problems, the United States Department of Agriculture established a Food Science Mission which traveled abroad in the fall of 1963 in an effort to determine the extent to which science played a role in developing these restrictions. It is hoped that a better understanding of these problems will be helpful in finding ways to eliminate some of the many "health hazard" bans.

Private Trade Activities

Private U.S. exporters of poultry and poultry products and their trade associations have worked with foreign importing associations to develop markets for poultry and eggs.

Market surveys, carried on by private and non-governmental agencies interested in poultry market development, have often served as a guide with respect to areas of need and methods for carrying out effective FAS market development programs. Their findings have been made available for immediate use in developing commercial business and for longer-term development projects.

Exporters of poultry products have participated privately, and through their associations, in international trade fairs. They have offered their assistance in presenting the story of progress of the U.S. poultry industry and in introducing and demonstrating a wide variety of U.S. ready-to-cook poultry and egg products.

President Lyndon B. Johnson, then Vice President, opened the U.S. Food and Agriculture Exhibition at Amsterdam, the Netherlands, November 25, 1963 , and was welcomed to the poultry booth by the American chef.

Trade Fairs

International fairs and expositions sponsored by the U.S. Departments of Agriculture and Commerce have proved to be an effective means of attracting officials of foreign governments, trade, and processors alike to learn about the quality, abundance, and reasonable prices of U.S. poultry products and to see U.S. production methods, processing, and marketing. In addition to stimulating local trade groups' interest in marketing techniques, these fairs have stimulated interest in importing poultry breeding stock. Frequently, demonstrations of feeding, processing, packaging, distribution, and educational exhibits were featured at international fairs. These exhibits have done much to pave the way for subsequent market development activities.

In 1963, this Division, in cooperation with the poultry industry, participated in trade fairs in the Netherlands, Germany, Italy, Peru, and Japan.

Market Information

To aid export market activities designed to expand exports of U.S. poultry and poultry products, FAS publishes periodically circulars covering trends in foreign production, U.S. and world trade and related information by principal countries. Current information received from U.S. Agricultural Attaches which may be of interest to exporters is released in the weekly Foreign Agriculture Magazine.

9

Following is a list of poultry and egg circulars published in 1963:

FPE 1-63 World Trade in Poultry Meat and Egg Products Up, February

FPE 2-63 U.S. Trade in Poultry and Eggs, 1962, August

FPE 3-63 World Trade in Poultry Meat and Eggs, 1962, October

DAIRY PRODUCTS AND DAIRY CATTLE

Foreign trade prospects for U.S. dairy products in the year immediately ahead appear favorable. While it is not expected that exports of butter will match the record high reached in 1963, shipments during the early months of 1964 should continue at relatively high levels. As long as U.S. butter is priced competitively, and the country's exporters continue to follow aggressive marketing practices, U.S. dairy products, particularly butter, will continue to move into new and expanding markets.

The prospects for expanded sales of U.S. dairy cattle in 1964 are good. Intensive promotional work carried on by FAS and the breed associations has succeeded in overcoming some of the many problems facing U.S. exporters. It is expected that U.S. exports of dairy cattle in 1964 will probably exceed 1963 shipments.

CURRENT WORLD SITUATION

World milk production in 1963 was down, interrupting for the second time in the last five years the upward trend in production evidenced during the past decade. Production in 35 countries, which normally account for about 85 percent of total world output, was down 2 percent. Production in these countries totaled about 606 billion pounds compared with 619 billion in 1962. The 1963 decline was caused by a combination of factors, mainly a drop in milk cow numbers, unfavorable weather in several areas, and generally higher feed prices. Slight declines in output took place in North America and in Western Europe. In Eastern Europe and the USSR, however, production was reported to have been off sharply because of a prolonged drought and short feed supplies.

As a consequence of the fall in total milk production, the quantity available for manufacturing purposes also declined. Output of butter--the item most severely affected--was estimated at 10.6 billion pounds, down about 3 percent from 1962. Cheese production was moderately higher. The switch to greater emphasis on cheese production came about because of a conscious effort in several countries to shift more milk from the manufacture of butter, a chronic surplus item in recent years, to cheese. In contrast to the situation for butter, demand for cheese has been steadily rising in recent years. The shift from butter to cheese was only partially successful because lower milk production, generally, reduced total supplies available for manufacturing purposes. However, total cheese production in 1963 was up about 1 percent from 1962.

Output of canned and dried whole milk was basically unchanged from the relatively low level of 1962. Production of nonfat dry milk, although closely tied to butter production, continued to increase. Declines in the

United States, the major producing country, were more than offset by greatly expanded output in Western Europe (France and West Germany, in particular), where additional drying facilities have recently been installed.

INTERNATIONAL TRADE

Butter

World trade in dairy products in 1963 was up sharply. Despite quota limitations on butter shipments into the United Kingdom and other significant importing countries, total trade in butter registered a moderate gain. Increased world butter trade was in part caused by a decline in production in Northern Europe, which was forced to import larger-than-average quantities. In the United Kingdom, butter supplies were running low by mid-year. Butter stocks were down because of a decline in domestic output; consumption was at a high level and some European suppliers had fallen behind on deliveries under their quota authorizations. Faced with a tight supply situation, the United Kingdom began to liberalize quota allotments, first to traditional suppliers, then to North America. Also, butter imports from the United States and Canada were liberalized to other Western European markets. The imported butter was used to meet domestic market requirements, thus making it possible for some countries that are important suppliers on the U.K. market to fulfill their quotas. Thus, U.S. butter exports played an important role in maintaining a reasonably stable price for butter in Western Europe during 1963.

Cheese

The volume of trade in cheese was about unchanged from the previous year. In many of the major producing countries, domestic demand continued to rise and international trade in cheese remained highly selective and oriented toward traditional patterns.

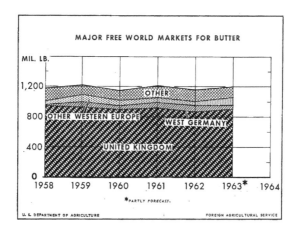

MAJOR FREE WORLD MARKETS FOR BUTTER

MIL. LB.

1,200

OTHER

800 — OTHER WESTERN EUROPE — WEST GERMANY

400 — UNITED KINGDOM

0
1958   1959   1960   1961   1962   1963*   1964

*PARTLY FORECAST.

U. S. DEPARTMENT OF AGRICULTURE   FOREIGN AGRICULTURAL SERVICE

11

Canned Milk

Trade in canned milk was up, mainly because of increased demand in the developing countries of Africa. Exports of nonfat dry milk continued to rise. Larger shipments from the United States to supply expanding demand for this product in school lunch and welfare programs was the principal factor responsible for this development. Indications point to a further decline in milk production in 1964. Lower milk cow numbers, feed shortages in many areas, and generally higher feed prices will make it difficult to reverse the downward trend in output during the next several months. Because of sizable stocks of butter and dried milk on hand in the United States and Canada, world trade in dairy products should continue at a high level, but higher prices may tend to restrain demand during 1964.

UNITED STATES IN THE WORLD SITUATION

Commercial exports of dairy products by the United States are likely to remain small, accounting for only a small part of domestic production. Because of increased production of bulk fresh and processed milk in Venezuela, our markets for dry whole milk there will probably decline. Our exports of canned milk also are likely to decline under competition from plants in the Philippines producing filled milk. Even though the potential market for dairy products in developing countries is enormous, (per capita milk consumption on a milk equivalent basis in many of these countries is estimated to be about one-tenth of per capita consumption in countries with advanced dairy industries) most developing countries cannot afford to import dairy products. Because of the shortage of foreign exchange and the export programs of other countries with advanced dairy industries, our exports of dairy products will depend almost entirely on the nature and extent of our special export programs. If the supply and consumption prospects described materialize, there will likely be an urgent need to continue donations and other special export programs at a high level.

Fluid Milk

Milk production in the United States in 1963 totaled 124.7 billion pounds, down about 1 percent from the record level of the previous year. Milk cow numbers were down about 3 percent, thus continuing the downtrend in dairy cattle in evidence for two decades. Reduced output, coupled with increased sales of fluid milk, resulted in lower purchases of dairy products by Commodity Credit Corporation (CCC) for price support purposes. CCC acquisitions in terms of milk equivalent during the 1963-64 marketing year have been estimated at about 6.8 billion pounds, compared with 8.3 billion pounds in 1962-63.

Nonfat Milk

Direct purchases of nonfat dry milk during the marketing year (April 1963 - March 1964) are expected to total 900 million pounds, compared with the purchases of 1.3 billion pounds during the same period for 1962-63. It is estimated that an additional 240 million pounds of nonfat will move into export channels under the payment-in-kind program. This compares with a total of 24 million pounds which moved in 1962-63.

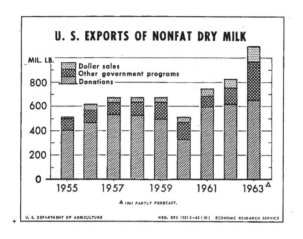

U. S. EXPORTS OF NONFAT DRY MILK

MIL. LB.

Dollar sales
Other government programs
Donations

△ 1963 PARTLY FORECAST.

U. S. DEPARTMENT OF AGRICULTURE   NEG. ERS 1321 X-63 (10)   ECONOMIC RESEARCH SERVICE

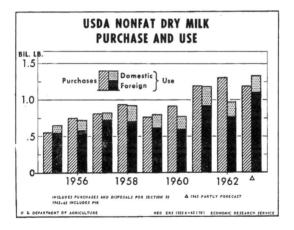

USDA NONFAT DRY MILK PURCHASE AND USE

BIL. LB.

Purchases   Domestic } Use
            Foreign

INCLUDES PURCHASES AND DISPOSALS FOR SECTION 32   △ 1963 PARTLY FORECAST
1962-63 INCLUDES PIK

U. S. DEPARTMENT OF AGRICULTURE   NEG ERS 1322 X-63 (10)   ECONOMIC RESEARCH SERVICE

13

Butter

U.S. exports of dairy products, particularly of butter, in calendar year 1963, were sharply higher. Because of the relatively high rate of production, large stocks of dairy products in CCC inventory at the beginning of 1963, and relatively limited export availabilities in the European surplus-producing countries, sizable quantities of U.S. butter were exported. U.S. butter and nonfat dry milk have been offered for export at competitive prices for the past several years, but most large commercial market outlets have been controlled by licensing and import quota arrangements. Thus, price has not been allowed to play the traditional free market role in establishing trade patterns. Numerous restrictive trade practices by all major butter importing countries, together with large quantities of product available for export in favored nations, have severely limited outlets for U.S. commercial sales.

The harsh winter experienced in Europe in 1963, and the resultant reduction in cattle numbers, higher prices for feed, and other factors contributed to a decline in butter production in several countries.

Reduced export availabilities in these countries provided United States and Canada the first opportunity in several years to move sizable quantities of butter into the European market. As a result, U.S. exports in calendar 1963 totaled about 80 million pounds. Approximately three-fourths of this total was destined for Europe. Exports of other dairy products were also higher but the gains were not so spectacular as in the case of butter.

Dairy Cattle

The value per head of U.S. dairy cattle exports in 1963 reached a record high, as average price rose for the fourth consecutive year, to over $400 each. The total value of exports was estimated at $5.3 million, up 3 percent from the previous record year of 1961.

The number of dairy cattle exported, however, did not surpass the abnormal high of 13,356 head in 1961 which was characterized by panic Cuban purchases of over 3,450 head before trade was embargoed. Considering the loss of this market, U.S. inspections for export in 1963 showed considerable gains as 12,599 head were shipped. This represents more than a 10 percent increase from 1962.

Mexico continued to be the largest market for U.S. dairy cattle, accounting for 73 percent of the total trade. Canada, our largest competitor for Latin American markets, was second, taking 1,146 head. Other major markets in order of importance were Venezuela, Dominican Republic, the Republic of the Philippines, and Korea.

The prime aim of the 1963 promotional activities was to increase exports to the established markets for dairy cattle in Central and South America. This goal was met, with sales to these areas about 25 percent greater than in 1962. The increase for Mexico alone was 30 percent. At the same time, work was intensified to cultivate greater sales in the Far East and Europe.

14

In Latin America, promotion followed a pattern proven successful over the years of extending maximum encouragement to foreign buyers. To help importing countries upgrade herds, U.S. breed representatives inspected and classified U.S. breeds and judged cattle in international livestock exhibitions.

A new source of financing dairy cattle exports was developed in 1963. It made it possible for U.S. exporters to get the Foreign Credit Insurance Association (FCIA) to insure loans for the purchase of U.S. cattle up to 85 percent of the loan value. It is expected that, through further expansion of this credit, sales can be increased further.

Besides Latin America, the United States expanded its sales to Japan and the Philippines, which together took over 270 head compared with only 13 in 1962. Following a series of marketing trips to Spain, that country purchased its largest shipment of U.S. dairy cattle to date. The groundwork was also laid for future sales of U.S. dairy cattle to Portugal, Italy, Morocco, and the Azores.

BUILDING WORLD MARKETS

Promotional Activity

In 1963, increased emphasis was placed on developing markets for U.S. dairy cattle and dairy products. Market survey work was intensified and expanded, especially into new areas, and much of it was directed to obtaining answers to specific marketing questions.

In 1963, an FAS marketing specialist and representatives of the five breed associations visited countries in Latin America, Spain, Morocco, and the Azores in efforts to expand the exports of dairy cattle. Much of the credit for increased dairy cattle exports in 1963 can be attributed to the work done by these specialists. They evaluated and summarized the nature and

Interest in purebred dairy cattle is promoted in Latin America through shows for which U.S. cattle associations some times provide judges. Here, Guillermo Jarrin, cattleman, U.S. Ambassador Maurice M. Bernbaum, and Carlos J. Ortega, U.S. agricultural attache, observe the Grand Champion Bull, in Ecuador.

15

extent of each country's current and prospective market for dairy cattle by breed, age and sex. By helping resolve trade complaints and by giving practical guidance in finding solutions for breeders' problems, they engendered considerable good will among producers.

During 1963, DSI expanded its cooperative market development activities through the establishment of two regional offices. In Chile where a small dairy recombining plant in Antofagasta has been supported through a promotional campaign, a full-time DSI employee was assigned to Santiago, and the earlier-restricted promotional campaign was expanded to a countrywide basis for all recombining plants using U.S. dairy ingredients to manufacture finished products.

Later in the year, DSI established a mid-East regional office in Lebanon to service projects in this area. DSI will endeavor to widen the use of milk products throughout the protein-short Middle East. Thus, the primary responsibility of this office will be encouragement to extend local milk supplies through use of imported nonfat dry milk, a procedure which has been successfully used in India. The first survey for implementation of this procedure has been undertaken in Egypt by DSI's Beirut representative.

The year 1963 marked the closing of the DSI dairy consumer-education program, in operation in Thailand since 1956. During that time, the project was active in promoting milk products to be included in the school lunch program, development of milk bars, and use of these products in commercial establishments. It was the aim of this project to build a permanent, commercial market for U.S. dairy products. This goal has been partially achieved, and the Thai's--who before 1956 were for the most part unfamiliar with most dairy products--have come to accept eagerly the new recombined products: ice cream, fluid milk, and flavored drinks. Because of the conviction that these objectives had been achieved and that future promotion could be handled entirely by existing dairies in Thailand, the project was terminated.

Dairy leaders and importers from nine countries, including Brazil, Chile, India, Iraq, Japan, Lebanon, Pakistan, the Philippines, and Spain were brought to the United States in June to attend the World Food Congress. These leaders represented a wide range of interests, but all indirectly concerned with purchase of dairy supplies for distribution through government or private channels. At the conclusion of the Congress, DSI arranged a tour of eight states where U.S. producers, processors, and exporters could meet with these foreign representatives and develop increased dairy product utilization and trade through personal discussions.

Another effort to further promote U.S. dairy products in Latin America took a Division and an industry representative to Peru. The team helped stimulate a desire for an FAS-DSI program similar to that being carried on in Chile.

Participation in Meetings

FAS representatives participated in both national and international dairy meetings during 1963. A representative attended the annual meetings of the

16

American Dry Milk Institute and American Dairy Association. Such activities are of a continuing nature.

In meetings of the joint FAO/WHO Codex Alimentarius Commission on Dairy Products, U.S. interests were represented.

Also, an FAS representative was a member of the official U.S. delegation that participated in an FAO meeting of experts on the "use of designations, definitions and standards for milk and milk products."

Overcoming Dollar Shortages

One way in which dollar shortages are being overcome is by the use of dollar export credits. The need for such credits for foreign buyers of U.S. dairy products and dairy cattle is acute, especially in the developing countries. Increasing inflation and falling foreign currency values which accompanied declining prices for raw materials, and the increasingly unfavorable position in which U.S. exporters found themselves as a result of the credit facilities offered by competing exporting countries, dictated the need for this credit.

Another means for overcoming dollar shortage is the U.S. Government programs designed for this purpose; namely the Agricultural Trade Development and Assistance Act of 1954 better known as Public Law 480. The fairly heavy exports of U.S. dairy products in recent years would not have been possible except for this program. Nonfat dry milk, butter, and cheese, all purchased by CCC for price support purposes, have been the leading dairy items exported under government programs. Particularly important has been Title III of P.L. 480, which authorizes CCC to donate surplus dairy products to voluntary relief organizations for free distribution to needy people in friendly foreign countries.

Private Trade Activities

Private U.S. exporters of dairy products and dairy cattle have continued efforts to enlarge or maintain existing foreign outlets and develop new ones, as well as to work with the cooperator organizations in fairs and in other FAS development projects. In support of the latter, they have participated actively in some trade fairs, furnished pictures, films and other educational and publicity material. They have on occasion conducted surveys at their own expense, aimed at direct market development and the solution of marketing problems, advising FAS of their findings. Dairy industry representatives have supported FAS marketing specialists in sales promotion for dairy products and cattle and in solving quality problems for the development of long-term markets. They have cooperated with FAS marketing specialists in supplying technical aid and advice on improved handling, storing, grading, displaying, packaging, and the use of other marketing devices.

17

Trade Fairs

DSI has been working with FAS through active participation in international trade fairs sponsored by the U.S. Departments of Agriculture and Commerce. These fairs have been important instruments for promoting and demonstrating the quality of U.S. dairy products. Fairs have also provided an effective means of demonstrating, to foreign governments and to trade, the excellent taste and reasonable cost of U.S. recombined milk, instant nonfat and chocolate milks, ice cream, and other products. Keen interest in U.S. dairy products and U.S. processing and distribution methods was evidenced at the Fine Foods Exhibit in Cologne, Germany. In 1963, this Division in cooperation with DSI participated in trade fairs in Berlin, Cologne and Lima, Peru.

At the U.S. Food Exhibit, ANUGA Fair, Cologne, West Germany, a young bilingual demonstrator in stars-and-stripes costume explains to German food importers how easy it is to mix a glass of chocolate milk from a package of nonfat dry powder.

Special Problems

Certain dairy items, such as butter and cheese, require refrigerated shipping and distribution facilities within the importing country. Such facilities are not always readily available in areas where the greatest potential market for dairy products exists. In some areas, educational work is required to acquaint the consumer with dairy products.

Market Information

For basic information relative to export markets for the principal dairy products, FAS has continued and extended its publication of circulars covering trends in foreign production and trade, and the conditions or limitations affecting such trade. Also, circulars summarizing U.S. exports of dairy cattle by sex, age group, U.S. state of origin, and country of destination are prepared.

Information received from marketing specialists and Agricultural Attaches, of interest to exporters of dairy products, is released weekly in the FAS publication, Foreign Agriculture.

The following is a list of all dairy circulars published in 1963:

FD 1-63 Per Capita Consumption of Dairy Products, 1960, 1961
         and indicated 1962   February

FD 2-63 World Trade in Dairy Products Up in 1961; Further
         Gains Expected in 1962   March

FD 3-63 U.S. Exports of Dairy Breeding Cattle, Preliminary
         Report 1962   April

FD 4-63 World Output of Dairy Products Increased in 1962   May

FD 5-63 Milk Production and Utilization in Principal Countries
         in 1962   July

FD 6-63 Butter and Cheese Production Up in 1962   July

FD 7-63 United States Dairy Exports Up in 1962   September

FD 8-63 World Trade in Dairy Products, 1961 and 1962   November

FD 9-63 World Milk Production Down 2 Percent in 1963   December

FD 10-63 World Output of Dairy Products Down Slightly in First
         Half of 1963   December

UNITED STATES DEPARTMENT OF AGRICULTURE

WASHINGTON, D. C. 20250

Official Business

National Milk Prod. Fed.
8-18-60 30 F St., N. W.
FD-C Washington 1, D. C.

CPSIA information can be obtained
at www.ICGtesting.com
Printed in the USA
LVHW021509261118
598291LV00012B/1203